Original title:
Into the Island Breeze

Copyright © 2025 Creative Arts Management OÜ
All rights reserved.

Author: Nora Sinclair
ISBN HARDBACK: 978-1-80581-596-9
ISBN PAPERBACK: 978-1-80581-123-7
ISBN EBOOK: 978-1-80581-596-9

Sandcastles of Lost Dreams

On the shore we make our stand,
With buckets, shovels, and much sand.
A castle grand, so tall and proud,
Then swoosh! It's gone, we laugh aloud.

The tide rolls in with sneaky glee,
Our turrets splash in salty spree.
We chase the waves, then trip and fall,
Tangled in nets, we have a ball.

Seagulls caw with mocking cries,
As our dreams wash by, oh what a surprise!
With every wave, a story told,
Of castles made, and laughter bold.

Oh, what joy this sandy quest,
Each grain a memory, the very best.
Though castles fade, we still can play,
Life's but a sand game, hip-hip-hooray!

The Pulse of Nature's Heart

Leaves rustle as we dance around,
A chorus sung, without a sound.
Wiggling worms, quite unplanned,
Join our jig across the land.

Breezy whispers, tickling cheeks,
Nature's giggles, oh so sleek.
Flowers laugh in colors bright,
While bees buzz tunes with pure delight.

A squirrel snickers from his branch,
With every step, a tiny chance.
Raccoons peek with curious eyes,
Joining the fun with playful sighs.

So let us pluck the sweetest fruit,
With nature's rhythm, we'll dance tooot!
Life's pulse beats strong with every cheer,
Let's toast to laughter and a cold beer!

Illusions Cast by the Setting Sun

The sun dips low, it starts to glow,
A crab waltzes by, slow like a pro.
Seagulls squawk, in a fancy dance,
Sandy feet slip, oh what a chance!

Flip-flops fly in the gentle air,
Someone's salad—no, that's a hair!
Laughter erupts like a wave on shore,
Sunburns and giggles, who could ask for more?

Visions of Twilight at the Cove

Twilight falls on kooky folks,
With glow stick bracelets and silly jokes.
A fish jumps high, perhaps to cheer,
While kids yell loudly, 'Make it clear!'

The bonfire crackles, marshmallows toast,
Someone sings off-key, but they love it most.
A raccoon grins, eyes all aglow,
Stealing chips as they put on a show.

Rituals in the Lagoon

In the lagoon, a splashy spree,
Ducklings paddle like they're set free.
A coconut falls, thud—what a sight,
The limbo stick bows; oh what a night!

Laughter erupts in a bubbly wave,
Friendships form with a giggly save.
Silly hats worn, not a care in sight,
Floating dreams under the moonlight.

Language of Waves and Palm Trees

Waves go hush, then whisper loud,
Palm trees sway, they're dancing proud.
A beach ball bounces here and there,
Chasing it down? Oh, what a dare!

The sun sets low, shadows play tricks,
In flip-flops, folks trying funny kicks.
Sandy noses and salty air,
Who knew fun could be so rare?

Secrets of the Palm Grove

A parrot steals my sandwich,
While I sip on coconut cream.
Monkeys laugh like old school pals,
Planning heists, it seems a dream.

Sandy toes in flip-flops worn,
Crabs scuttle by, winking at me.
They know more than they let on,
Whispers of beach-life jubilee.

Giggling waves and frothy wine,
A sea cucumber plays the fool.
Tickling my toes with ocean's rhyme,
In this grove, we all play cool.

Dreaming in a Salted Dusk

Seagulls argue over fries,
As the sun begins to dive.
Sandy shenanigans arise,
In this beachy, silly hive.

Footprints lead to nowhere fast,
A crab snaps at my floating hat.
Whispered jokes in shadows cast,
The ocean's got a wicked spat.

Laughter echoes, waves collide,
Shells tell tales of starlit nights.
Every heartbeat, joy, and pride,
In this dusk, all feels so right.

Voyage to the Coral Horizon

I sail on a banana boat,
With a dolphin, oh so spry.
He flips, I slip, we share a joke,
As salty tears flow from my eye.

Turtles dance in slow-mo grace,
While clams compete for best-dressed prize.
A starfish waves with clumsy pace,
Beneath a sea of endless skies.

A treasure chest of silly dreams,
Buried deep in bubbly foam.
Laughing hard, the world redeems,
On this voyage, we're at home.

Tides of a Forgotten Paradise

Naps on beach towels in a heap,
While crickets sing their murky tune.
Sandy castles start to creep,
As the sun dips, we're over the moon.

Waves come in with playful grins,
To tickle toes and splash the shy.
Laughter echoes, the fun begins,
In this paradise, we all fly high.

Seashells chuckle at our plight,
As we chase them down the shore.
With each tide, we feel delight,
Forgotten shores, forevermore.

Beneath the Canopy of Stars

Under the sky where the wishes roam,
A squirrel just claimed my beach chair as home.
With one tiny nut, all my snacks he swipes,
I shout, 'You thief!' as he giggles and types.

Tidal waves laughing, they dance on the shore,
While seagulls barge in, looking for more.
A crab took my flip-flop; what a funny sight,
He wears it with style, all day and all night.

Odyssey on Sunlit Waters

A boat full of friends, we drift on the sea,
One paddles with flair, the other with glee.
I thought I was smooth, but I fell with a splash,
And now my big hat's a mermaid's mustache.

The dolphins are laughing, they jump in delight,
While I'm busy dodging my sunscreen fight.
The seagulls point fingers, they squawk with a shout,
As if they all know what I'm flailing about.

Embrace of Coastal Shadows

Under palm trees swaying, I try to read,
But the wind grabs my pages like it's got greed.
I chase them down, shouting, 'Hey, come back here!'
As they dance with the breeze, I'm stuck in my gear.

A turtle crawls past, looking mighty confused,
While I'm fanning my face, feeling quite used.
He chuckles and plods on, moving real slow,
I bet he's got tales of sunburns to show.

Lullaby of the Distant Waves

As night falls, my friends pull out their old tunes,
Strumming guitars beneath the bright moons.
Each note mixes laughter with mischief galore,
When one sings off-key, we all hit the floor.

The waves start to tap dance, splashing along,
As crickets join in, making their song.
With marshmallows roasting, and jokes in the air,
Who knew evenings like this would be so rare?

Secrets Carried on the Wind

The parrots squawk secrets so bold,
While coconut palms tell tales of old.
A crab in a tux, with a wink and a grin,
Paces on the shore as the laughter begins.

A breeze brings whispers of silly pranks,
As seagulls conspire in playful flanks.
Fish flip-flop, causing such a scene,
While sandcastles wave like a beachside queen.

A flip-flop giggle, a playful jest,
The sun starts dancing, as it does best.
With every gust, a tickle for all,
On this sunny day, let good times befall.

Radiance of the Setting Sun

Golden rays chuckle as daylight fades,
While shadows perform in sun-soaked parades.
Jellyfish wear hats like they're ready to shine,
And dolphins throw parties, sipping on brine.

The sun sneezes sparkles, a glittery haze,
Balloons float by in a pastel daze.
With each wave that crashes, laughter will swell,
Echoing echoes of secrets to tell.

Children chase fireflies, a flickering chase,
Their giggles and shrieks fill each sandy space.
As the horizon stretches, the sun starts to yawn,
The day's hilarious memories linger on.

Horizons of Uncharted Dreamscapes

Sailing on clouds made of cotton candy,
With jellybean stars that are simply dandy.
Adventure awaits on a floaty delight,
A mermaid sings limericks, oh what a sight!

Explorers in flip-flops, with maps upside down,
Search for treasures lost beyond the town.
Pirates on surfboards steal tumbling waves,
While llamas in sunglasses are barely saved.

Sandy-haired kittens chase shadows so bold,
Dancing on beaches where stories unfold.
Every corner giggles with surprises in store,
In these wild dreamscapes, we forever explore.

Soft Footprints on Warm Sands

Little feet make patterns that giggle and sway,
As they run through the beach on a bright sunny day.
A sprightly hermit crab joins in the fun,
Clapping his claws, all day long he'll run.

Footprints fade softly, like jokes lost in time,
Leaving behind traces, a warm sandy rhyme.
Bubbles pop loudly, a playful uproar,
As wave after wave keeps asking for more.

Each grain of sand knows a story to tell,
From picnics and laughs to the splash of a shell.
On this sandy canvas, life dances along,
With light as our melody, fun is our song.

Rhythm of the Gentle Swell

Seagulls dance and squawk a tune,
As waves tickle toes in the afternoon.
Surfboards wobble, folks shout with glee,
A crab sneaks in, it's baiting me!

The sun hangs low, casting golden rays,
Flip-flops fly in the silliest ways.
Kids build castles, one foot at a time,
While a dog swipes all snacks - oh, what a crime!

Laughter echoes along the shore,
Where sunscreen fights are never a bore.
An old man stumbles, hat flies away,
And fish laugh hard, at the human ballet!

Tanned skin glistens with salt and fun,
Chasing ice cream carts, they all run.
Life is a joke, with some sandy twists,
As the tide rolls in, we can't resist!

Sunlit Paths on Sandy Shores

Sunshine beams on every face,
As beachgoers fall in a race.
Toward the sea with a splash and a cry,
While auntie's hat sails high in the sky!

Picnics sprawled, with sandwiches rare,
Sandwiches? More like mysterious layers!
Ants march in with a picnic heist,
While chips and dip are at utter risk!

Kites soar high, they dance and tease,
Getting tangled in palm trees with ease.
Kids run by, with laughter so loud,
Oh, to be free as a sunbeam cloud!

Beach balls collide in a goofy brawl,
While a toddler wobbles, about to fall.
Old folks chuckle at the sight so sweet,
On sunlit paths, life's a playful treat!

Haven of Lapping Waters

The waves tickle toes, a watery mess,
Where every splash brings giggles, no less.
Old folks nap while kids take a dive,
In this haven of chaos, we feel so alive!

Sun hats float like boats in the sea,
As sunscreen artists paint limbs with glee.
A seagull steals someone's last fry,
Oh, the comedy in every heartfelt sigh!

Floating on noodles, they sip their drinks,
While mermaids dance, or so the kid thinks.
Beach chairs topple like castles of sand,
Ensuring that fun is always at hand!

With laughter and snacks, we wade near the shore,
Chasing waves as they dance and roar.
Life's punchlines land with a splashy cheer,
In these lapping waters, joy draws near!

Twilight Dreams on Distant Shores

As twilight falls and colors mix,
The sand castles look like ruins and tricks.
Laughter echoes as we roast the s'mores,
With marshmallows flying, oh, what a score!

Ghost stories told as shadows creep,
While the ocean whispers secrets to keep.
A sudden wave drenches the wild crew,
Leaving behind drenched fears and boo-hoo!

Starry skies glitter, and crabs strut proud,
While the moonlight breaks through a playful cloud.
Scooters zoom by, leaving trails of gleam,
As friends unite in a whimsical dream!

In this twilight glow, fun is a game,
Where every moment feels like a flame.
With hearts so light, we dance on the shore,
In these distant dreams, we always want more!

Bliss Beneath the Coconut Canopy

Underneath the tall green trees,
I dance with shadows in the breeze.
Coconuts drop; I deftly dodge,
I might just need a coconut lodge.

With laughter ringing, there I sway,
The crabs all join the dance, hooray!
A seagull steals my snack right then,
I'll plot my snack revenge again.

A hammock swings, it's like a dream,
But then I spill my fruit juice cream.
While breezes tease my wrinkled hat,
I'm giggling like an old-time cat.

So here I'll stay, sun on my toes,
With silly games, my laughter flows.
In coconut shade, where joy is clear,
Life's a joke, let's laugh and cheer!

Notes Carried by the Ocean's Breath

Waves bring messages from afar,
They whisper tales beneath the star.
A crab's long dance makes quite the scene,
It's a shellfish show, fit for a queen.

Seagulls squawk a comical tune,
While beach balls bounce and swim like a loon.
I let the salt tease at my nose,
As seashells giggle, who really knows?

I try to ride a wave so bold,
But end up flopping, truth be told.
The dolphins laugh as I wipe sand,
The ocean's breath lends a helping hand.

So here I sit, with seashells in tow,
Trading sea tales, letting them flow.
The breeze carries laughs and not regrets,
As I pen notes, no real requirements yet!

Journey of the Wandering Shell

A shell sets off, it starts to roam,
On sandy trails, it finds a home.
With little feet, it tiptoes past,
Learning that travel's quite a blast.

Through giggles and sand, it slides away,
From crabs debating who'll win today.
It tumbles and rolls, not one bit shy,
"What's that over there?" it asks the sky.

Each wave that breaks is a comedy show,
Where fish tell jokes just below the flow.
Though it feels lost, it's on a quest,
To find the laughter that's truly best.

So on it glides with a smile so bright,
Making friends in the warm sunlight.
A journey that twists, a tale to tell,
Life's more fun with a wandering shell.

A Breeze That Whispers Freedom

A gentle gust stirs all in sight,
Scooting my hat, what a flight!
It nudges the palm fronds, oh what fun,
In this playful place, we all just run.

The breeze invites all to join its chase,
A tumble here, a laugh at pace.
I chase my napkin, what a scene,
My beach day's comedy, oh so keen.

It twirls around as I chase my toes,
With wavy hair and ice cream woes.
While seagulls laugh, flapping away,
I'll take the breeze 'til the end of the day.

So let's embrace this light, sweet air,
With goofy moments and sun-kissed flair.
In the dance of joy we all pursue,
A breeze of laughter, just me and you!

Beneath the Canopy of Stars

Under twinkling lights so bright,
I tripped on sand, what a sight!
A crab with swagger scuttled near,
Said, "Watch your step, my friend, not here!"

A rocket flew, a bird did squawk,
As people danced and took a walk.
With laughter high and worries low,
We shared our dreams, not one in tow.

The night confessed its silly tales,
Of whispered winds and playful gales.
My friend discovered her flip-flop's fate,
Now it's a crab's new home to sate!

As we sat lost in roaring waves,
Each splash became the joke that saves.
Beneath this sky, so vast and free,
The stars could laugh right back at me.

The Ebb and Flow of Nightfall

The tide danced in with shimm'ring glee,
The moon a spotlight for fish to see.
I pondered how jellyfish felt,
Floating in gobs, as if they melted.

The night we laughed at seaweed's plight,
Who could've thought it'd start a fight?
"Let's wrestle now!" one seagull cried,
But landed wrong, flapped off and sighed.

Waves whispered secrets, quite absurd,
I heard a clownfish mutter a word.
"Can I borrow your sunglasses, please?"
"Only if you share some ocean breeze."

As shadows stretched and giggles beat,
The horizon offered my sandy seat.
Just a night of pure balmy cheer,
Where laughter rang and floated near.

Currents of Forgotten Conversations

We sat upon rocks, drinks in tow,
Debating if jellyfish really glow.
With each wave came a story told,
Mixing with laughter, fortunes bold.

A dolphin jumped, quite the surprise,
While we puzzled at fish in disguise.
One claimed fins could actually chat,
"If they can talk, please call a cat!"

The breeze played tricks, tossed hair around,
My hat flew off, I chased it down.
"Does the ocean have hat insurance?"
"No, but it's signed up for sea-surance!"

Who knew the waves held so much fun?
With tides that sparkled like a gun.
We drifted off on currents sweet,
And waved goodbye with sandy feet.

Poetics of a Sun-Drenched Shore

A sun-kissed morning, what a flair,
With beach balls bouncing everywhere.
Veggies trying to tan on sand,
But passing seagulls had another plan!

A sandcastle stood, proud and tall,
Till a wave arrived, its curtain call.
"Dear wall," I claimed, "stay strong and brave!"
It crumbled down, then I misbehaved!

The surf sang songs of frolic and cheer,
My flip-flops vanished, witness near.
Now mismatched footwear's all the rage,
"No one's foot should be in a cage!"

With laughter floating on warm seashells,
We chased the sun, and shared our yells.
"Let's race!" we screamed, as we ran fast,
To find the shore and make joy last.

Embracing Nature's Gentle Breath

A cat on a surfboard, what a sight,
Waves roll by, giving quite a fright.
Seagulls cackle, the sun does dance,
As crabs do their tango, take a chance.

The breeze swirls round with playful tease,
Whispers of laughter among the trees.
Fish in the sea join in the fun,
Diving for snacks, just for a pun.

Turtles wearing hats, so debonair,
Join in the revelry without a care.
Butterflies giggle, flapping their wings,
While squirrels plot pranks, oh, the joy it brings.

So here we bask in this giddy place,
Nature's mischief has a silly face.
A toast to the whimsy that fills the air,
In this joyful chaos, there's love to share.

The Allure of Endless Blue

Why do the fish seem to wear a grin?
Could it be laughter? Let's dive in!
Dolphins are juggling, not one, but two,
While the crabs throw shells at the big fish crew.

The ocean waves tease with a playful curl,
Nature's own stand-up, watch it unfurl.
Sandy toes tickle, as frolic ensues,
Splashing about in fun summer hues.

Seagulls drop snacks like confetti in flight,
In a clam-shell party, the mood feels just right.
A mermaid shows off her dance from the reef,
With a twirl and a splash, it's pure comic relief.

So join in the laughter, let's swim and sway,
Under the sun, let's make every day.
With waters so bright and skies of pure hue,
Life here is better, it's laughter anew.

Sails of the Soul in Serene Waters

A boat with a captain who likes to sing,
Swabbing the deck, he's a one-man fling.
Sails are all tattered, like worn-out jeans,
But he claims they're stylish, if you know what he means.

The wind plays tricks, it shimmies and shakes,
He offers a dance with his boat for mates.
Fish rolling by, wishing they could sway,
While whispers of dreams float away in play.

The sun sets low, making shadows all long,
He strums on the hull, humming a song.
Seagulls soar high, join in the tune,
While pirates below try to find a balloon.

But worry not, for here we are free,
Riding the waves with giggles and glee.
In this silly voyage, joy always wins,
With sails full of laughter, the journey begins.

The Tapestry of Sea and Sky

Clouds shaped like bunnies drift thin and wide,
Fish in the water join in the ride.
A whale wearing glasses slurps down a drink,
And winks at the octopus, "What do you think?"

Colors of sunset paint funny old tales,
As critters come out with their quirky scales.
A flamingo on stilts thinks he's a star,
While the pelicans debate who's the best at guitar.

As night rolls in, stars giggle and gleam,
The moon tries to dance, but it can't find the dream.
With lanterns of jellyfish lighting the way,
Nature's own library, where critters do play.

So gather around, let's weave all our cheer,
In the fabric of laughter, hold friendships dear.
As waves crash forth, let's not miss a beat,
In this playful harmony, life's truly sweet.

Twilight Serenade by the Sea

The sun dips low, a golden tease,
As I trip over my own two knees.
A seagull laughs, it steals my snack,
  I wonder if it'll bring it back.

The waves clap hands, a joyful cheer,
I dance like no one else is near.
The crab scuttles, it looks quite sly,
  I wink at it as it hurries by.

The stars come out, they start to glow,
While I ponder if I should just go.
But wine from coconuts, oh so sweet,
Makes this silly dance feel quite complete.

With laughter echoing in the night,
I trip on sand, then take to flight.
The moon beams down, a silver swish,
I call for dolphins, but it's just my dish.

Tranquil Thoughts on Tropical Breezes

A gentle wind, it pulls my hair,
I wonder if it's done with care.
It whispers secrets, oh so bold,
While I sit here, feeling cold.

The palm trees sway in silly dance,
I join them too—give it a chance!
A parrot shouts, "What's up, my friend?"
I reply, "Just looking for a trend!"

The beach ball rolls, I chase it down,
And end up wearing sand like a crown.
The fish below seem to giggle too,
As they plot my next great to-do.

Oh, thoughts of fun fill up the air,
As I ponder life without a care.
A lounge chair calls, time for a rest,
Tomorrow's plans, I'll keep them guessed.

The Harmony of Seashells and Gulls

Seashells sing, a charming tune,
While gulls parade beneath the moon.
I try to dance, but slip and slide,
With shells as maracas by my side.

The tide rolls in, splashes my toes,
The seagulls cackle at my woes.
They steal my lunch, and with a squawk,
Leave me to sway and fortune-walk.

Each shell I find tells a joke or two,
Of cocktails served and what to do.
The waves roll laughter on repeat,
As I trip backward, oh, what a feat!

In this orchestra of sun and sand,
Laughter dances, takes a stand.
With every wave, a splashy giggle,
Life here is one big, joyful wiggle.

Navigating the Quiet Waters of Reflection

My boat floats on a sea of thought,
But where's my snack? It's all for naught!
The fish below, they give a grin,
As I ponder where to begin.

The oars are missing, lost, I fear,
I wave to dolphins, bring me cheer!
They jump and twirl, so full of grace,
While I just float in this silly place.

My cap is lost to the ocean's sway,
The sun just laughs, it's quite a day.
I'll sip my drink, with ice—so cool!
And try my best not to be a fool.

In the calm where worries fade,
I search for peace but find a parade.
With every splash, I shed a frown,
Laughing now, I'll never drown!

Twilight Echoes in the Tropics

As the sun dips low, a bird sings loud,
Crickets join in, forming quite the crowd.
A monkey swings from a palm tree high,
Chasing shadows that dance in the sky.

A turtle named Bob tried to dance a jig,
He twisted and turned, quite the amusing dig.
The flamingos chuckle, all in a row,
While waves tap their feet, putting on a show.

A breeze hums a tune, soft and so clear,
While seagulls gossip, bringing good cheer.
The sunset paints colors, a brush full of fun,
As the day whispers softly, "Hey, we're not done!"

So raise up a drink, let laughter resound,
In this tropical twilight, joy can be found.
With each little giggle, and sun's final bow,
We're dancing on clouds in the warm evening now.

Sanctuary of the Coastal Heart

In a hammock that sways like a fish in a stream,
I drift off to dreams, lost in a gleam.
A crab scuttles by, wearing a hat,
While dolphins perform dances, imagine that!

Palm trees are swaying, tickling the sand,
As laughter erupts from the merry band.
A parrot named Lou, with a flair for the jest,
Tells corny old jokes, he's truly the best.

The sun spills its secrets, bright like a show,
Turtles nod along, moving nice and slow.
An octopus juggles with shells, it's a sight,
While a sea turtle rolls, grinning with delight.

As evening draws near, fireflies will gleam,
Making wishes come true, or so it would seem.
With stars overhead and laughter to share,
This sanctuary calls, beyond all compare.

Nature's Warm Embrace

Beneath the warm sun, a squirrel plays chess,
With a coconut really, no need to impress.
The waves laugh aloud, tickling the shore,
While crabs take selfies, always wanting more.

A breeze tickles noses, causing a sneeze,
While pelicans strut with such casual ease.
They'll tell you a tale of the fish they once caught,
Except that the wise ones were always too fraught.

The rain drops for tea, a soft little pat,
While turtles do backflips, wearing a hat.
The flora joins in, with a wink and a swirl,
As bees do a tango, giving it a twirl.

Under the sky, with giggles the air,
Nature's warm embrace is beyond all compare.
With joy in each moment, a laugh in each ray,
We dwell in the fun, come join in the play.

Tranquility Under the Coconut Skies

Beneath the tall palms, dreams dance like fire,
While geckos recite lines, never to tire.
The ocean is chuckling, waves rolling in,
With whispers of mischief, where shall I begin?

A dolphin named Sue tried to sing a tune,
While crabs joined the chorus, under the moon.
Tropical breezes tickling the grass,
Every rustle and giggle, a reason to laugh.

The stars winking down, a celestial crowd,
They chuckle together, so happy and proud.
As the sun takes a bow, it splashes with glee,
Nature's own party, come join, it's free!

With each silly moment, we twirl and we sway,
In this paradise found, we cherish each day.
So raise up a drink and toast to delight,
Under coconut skies, everything feels right.

Embrace of the Shoreline

A crab in a tux, what a sight to see,
Dancing with waves, so full of glee.
Seagulls squawk jokes, all in good fun,
As sunbathers chase after the sun.

The sand's a warm blanket, itchy but nice,
Kids build grand castles, then roll them like dice.
The tide comes in, as if on command,
Toppling towers made of soft golden sand.

A flip-flop thief steals your right shoe,
As the left one sits, confused and blue.
What's with the palm trees, swaying so free?
They argue their height—who's tallest? Not me!

But as the sun sets, the laughter will last,
With stories of crabs and flip-flops broadcast.
We'll toast to the moments, both silly and sweet,
In the embrace of this shoreline retreat.

Echoes in the Palm Fronds

Palm fronds whisper secrets, tales of the tide,
While tourists sip coconut drinks with great pride.
A parrot named Steve has a knack for a joke,
He mimics a laugh, then sends them up in smoke.

Beach balls are bouncing like fish out of sea,
While kids chase their dreams with a splash and a plea.
The sun is a jester, playing all tricks,
As sunscreen slips and your friend does the splits.

The hammock swings low, a sloth is in view,
Napping away, he dreams of a zoo.
But vision's a blur for a drink-blurred head,
When the only thing seen is the pool of red spread.

Echoes of laughter, from dusk until night,
We giggle and guffaw in the shimmering light.
The palms sway along, they can't help but sway,
As we make silly memories, come what may.

Serene Saltwater Sighs

Seagulls play poker, perched on a post,
As waves break the silence, hosting a toast.
The fish in the sea gossip in fins,
While sunbathers sport their most colorful skins.

The shells on the shore hold stories untold,
Of mermaids with hair woven from gold.
A flip-flop parade of mismatched footwear,
Floating through sand, what a sight, oh so rare!

But watch out for riptides, they come with a grin,
And sweep up your towel, your swimsuit—your twin!
We laugh at the chaos, our hearts full of cheer,
As the sunset spills colors, and brings a new year.

Saltwater sighs mixed with giggles and glee,
In the dance of the day, we're wild and carefree.
Each wave, a reminder of fun days gone past,
In the serene saltwater, our memories cast.

Dance of the Seafoam

At dawn, the seafoam wears a frothy crown,
Bobbing and weaving, it never looks down.
It tickles our toes, with a cheeky retreat,
While jellyfish float by, skipping their beat.

Beachvolley at noon, where the stakes are high,
One misjudged serve, and a sunhat will fly.
We dive for the ball, all laughter and flair,
Till the ref is a dolphin, giving a stare.

Shadows of sandcastles, crumbled and worn,
Crabs put on shows, tap-dancing till dawn.
Another splash fight starts, oh, what a grand call,
As the beach turns to chaos, we all take a fall.

And when the sun dips, the stories arise,
Of seafoam's great dance, stretching under the skies.
A night of good spirits, as stars twinkle bright,
In the dance of the seafoam, everything feels right.

Captivated by the Sunset Glow

The sun dips low, a bold display,
A cat chases shadows, in a playful sway.
Laughter erupts as seagulls squawk,
While beach balls fly, it's a wild talk.

Flip-flops lost in a sandy pit,
As a child giggles, not a care, a hit.
Sunblock's thick, a comical smear,
We toast to fun with a cold root beer.

A crab scuttles fast, a little thief,
Stealing pretzels, causing disbelief.
With sunburned noses and silly hats,
We dance like crabs, and that's just that!

As twilight falls, we share our woes,
Like run-away drinks and sticky toes.
The sunset glows with a golden grace,
We laugh at life, in this perfect place.

Nestled in Nature's Arm

In trees that sway, we find our cheer,
A squirrel's dance brings us near.
He steals my snack, with such bold flair,
While I just sit and pull my hair.

Bugs in the air, they twirl and tease,
I swat at them with a loud wheeze.
Nature's chorus sings a funny tune,
As I trip over roots, oh what a ruin!

The flowers giggle, the grass grows tall,
We set up camp, and find the ball.
A marshmallow fight, oh what a sight,
With embers popping, the flames ignite!

From hammy meatballs to sticky s'mores,
We feast like kings, then laugh on floors.
In nature's hug, we share our bliss,
Giggling folks, what could we miss?

Secrets Carried by Gentle Breezes

With whispers soft, the breeze does play,
It tells me secrets of the day.
A coconut falls with a loud thud,
Sending all of us into the mud.

A beach chair's flip, a clumsy fumble,
As someone tries to escape a tumble.
Sunscreen's slippery, what a sight,
Like oil on ice, oh what a fright!

Palm trees sway, dance like they're high,
While I attempt to reach for the sky.
A frisbee flies, goes the wrong way,
Hitting a dog—and he runs to play!

Laughter echoes with each sweet breeze,
As we enjoy our snacks with ease.
Secrets shared, with giggles abound,
Every moment, we lose or found.

Canvas of the Softest Skies

The clouds are fluffy, cotton candy dreams,
I point and shout, "Look! A whale with streams!"
A kite battles high against the puffs,
While a lizard does yoga, oh that's enough!

Picnic spills, oh what a mess,
Butterflies flutter, and we all guess.
Mismatched socks among the fun,
As we chase shadows, and dart in the sun.

With laughter loud, we jump with glee,
A tumbler rolls, it's as wild as can be.
A sibling's slip on a banana peel,
Leaves us all laughing, that's the real deal!

As the sun sets, we cradle dreams,
In a world where nothing's as it seems.
The canvas painted, with colors bright,
In funny moments, we find our light.

The Stillness Between Tides

A crab in a tux, he sips his drink,
While seagulls debate on what to think.
The shells play cards, a wild affair,
Whispers of salt float in the air.

The starfish dance with floppy glee,
As fish gossip over cups of tea.
A clam with shades, so chic and neat,
Shuffles his pearls with a tap on the feet.

But watch your step, there's muck around,
And seaweed wigs stuck to the ground.
A dolphin's joke echoes wide and loud,
As laughter bubbles up from the crowd.

So here we sit while the tide shifts slow,
Laughing at antics only we know.
In this stillness, a riotous game,
Where nature's humor is never the same.

Echoes of Distant Lighthouses

A lighthouse beams, but can't find its hat,
The waves tease it, making it splat.
Bright stripes of red with a smile so wide,
While a pelican jokes, "Come on, take a ride!"

The foghorn's laughter fills up the night,
While crabs perform their own funny plight.
With lanterns swinging from swaying trees,
The wind howls jokes that tickle the breeze.

Old sailors chuckle, lost in the mist,
They forget their age with a flick of their wrist.
Each echo bounces tales far and wise,
But can't seem to find their own disguise.

So let's make merry in the lighthouse glow,
Where every beam has a story to show.
If laughter lights the way we steer,
Then this harbor's home is always near.

Sailboats Against the Blushing Sunset

Sailboats dip, like ballet in pairs,
While a fish practices jazz with flare.
The sun blushes pink on this stage so wide,
As turtles mime, laughing with pride.

Wind's playfully swirling, a trickster dress,
Whispering secrets none can suppress.
The sails like smiley faces up high,
Wave at the gulls zooming by, oh my!

A rogue wave splashes, with a giggly swoosh,
As dolphins report with a joyful whoosh.
"With all these colors, who needs a stage?
Let's all be silly and flip this page!"

So here in these waters, fun takes its flight,
A symphony of chuckles, oh what a sight!
With sunset as backdrop, laughter will spread,
In this playful ocean, where worries are shed.

The Magic of Indigo Waters

Indigo dreams swim deep in the sea,
Where mermaids wear crowns made of jelly, you see.
They throw a party with bubbles and cheer,
While octopuses juggle without any fear.

A sea sponge DJ drops beats on the sand,
Fish flash their scales, forming a band.
And the sea turtles, so slow and grand,
Crack jokes about waves, always unplanned.

The starfish rock out without a care,
While clownfish giggle in a fishy affair.
With laughter like tides, flowing so free,
In these magical waters, it's all about glee.

So let's dive in, let the good times roll,
Where every splash is a happy shoal.
In the magic of deep blues, life's a dance,
Join in the fun, give laughter a chance!

The Calm After the Storm

The skies are clear, the sun is bright,
A seagull tries to take a bite.
My beach umbrella took a flight,
Chased by waves in sheer delight.

Hats are flying, laughter's loud,
Someone lost a flip-flop shroud.
Sandy shoulders, oh so proud,
Grinning in a sunny crowd.

A kid's down pouring buckets neat,
Caught in a dance, he skips his feet.
The ocean giggles, what a treat,
As jellyfish twirl to the beat.

With smoothies thrown like cannon shots,
Beach games turn to rigged-up plots.
An ice cream truck hits all the spots,
Who knew chaos could be such lots?

Tales of the Swaying Mangroves

In the shade of trees that twist and bend,
A crab scuttles, his only friend.
A pelican drops, aiming to blend,
While children giggle at each silly trend.

Swatting at flies, we share a laugh,
An old sea turtle takes a gaff.
He munches greens, the crafty calf,
In this wild world, he's the photograph.

The wind plays tricks, tugs at our hats,
A squirrel sneaks by with nuts and chats.
He judges us like mere diplomats,
Admiring sunscreen-coated chitchats.

Underneath the sway, we weave our tales,
Glancing at fish in swirling trails.
As daylight fades, our laughter sails,
In mangrove whispers, fun never fails.

Drifting on a Whispering Zephyr

A gentle breeze whispers my name,
It tickles my nose, oh what a game!
Twirling my hair, without a shame,
As a seagull squawks, so loud, so tame.

I lie on a raft, dreaming of flight,
While sipping punch, feeling just right.
A dolphin splashes, what a sight,
I yell, 'Hey buddy, keep it light!'

The sunshine dances on waves like jazz,
With swim trunks in air, I make a razz.
But then I slip, oh what a pizzazz,
Flopping around, in this beachy pizazz.

So here we float, silly and free,
On waves of laughter, just you and me.
As the breeze carries our friendly glee,
We drift through a day, as light as can be.

Floating Thoughts in Ocean Air

Thoughts like boats, they come and go,
On the sea of dreams, it's quite a show.
A seahorse grins, he steals the glow,
While a clam thinks, 'I'm not too slow!'

I ponder fish with hats and ties,
Would they dance if they could fly?
With dolphins as my alibi,
We plot to paint the stars and sigh.

A jellyfish winks, wearing a dress,
While other critters feel the stress.
Footprints on shores lead to mess,
But oh, the joy, I must confess!

So let the waves carry my dreams,
With sandy toes, I craft my schemes.
In ocean air, life's as it seems,
A floaty world, where laughter beams.

Daydreams Beneath an Endless Sky

On a cloud I sit and sigh,
Chasing seagulls that zoom by.
A sandwich lands upon my head,
Now I'm feasting, dreams instead!

Sunburned noses, loud and bright,
Diving in without a fright.
Flip-flops flying, laughter sings,
Swim trunks tie up like old strings.

An umbrella chases me around,
Like a friend who can't be found.
Boys with boogie boards take flight,
Wipeouts make for pure delight!

The waves are ticklish, what a tease,
Salty snacks bring giggles, wheeze!
Beneath this vast, absurd expanse,
I'll dance with crabs, given a chance!

The Soul's Journey Through Ocean Breeze

With flip-flops flopping, off I go,
Beneath the sun's warm, golden glow.
The tide pulls me, a gentle nudge,
I'm off to find my snacky grudge!

Seashells whisper, "Take a break!"
But I'm on the hunt—my lunch, I stake.
A sandwich swims away from me,
Alright, I guess it's lunch for free!

The sailboats wobble, I lose my hat,
Chasing it down, oh, how I spat!
Mermaids giggle, "What's your plan?"
I'm just a human, running fast as I can!

With ice cream dripping down my arm,
I trip over seaweed's hidden charm.
My soul takes flight on this wavy spree,
Embracing hiccups with pure glee!

Star Dappled Reflections on the Water

Stars above like playful pins,
Jumping in a game, it begins.
The moon is showing off tonight,
I think it knows it's shining bright!

Splashing water's a cheeky dance,
As fish give me their best glance.
I wave at shadows, they wave back,
In this shimmering, tranquil track.

Turtles tease with a gentle glide,
While my floaty starts to slide.
A frog in chorus sings away,
Making fun of my wet ballet!

Caught in bubbles, giggles flame,
"Whee!" I squeal, "This is the game!"
The night feels like a silly play,
Where laughter rules—hip, hip, hooray!

Kaleidoscope of Sunset Hues

Paintbrush skies of pink and gold,
Turn my thoughts to tales retold.
I wear my shades, look oh-so-slick,
While chasing sunsets, what a trick!

The sun's a baker, making pies,
As marshmallows fill up the skies.
I grab a scoop—what a delight,
I'll taste the sunset, day turns night!

Sailboats become hotdog boats,
Floating past with funny quotes.
A crab with shades gives me a wink,
As I ponder my next drink!

The colors clash, a loud parade,
While seagulls join in this escapade.
With hearty laughter, I lose track,
As nighttime whispers, "Don't look back!"

The Song of the Low Tide

The crab danced sideways with glee,
As the waves tucked in for the night.
A fish wearing glasses did see,
And promptly swam off in fright.

Seagulls arguing over hot fries,
Fighting like kids on a spree.
Sunburned tourists with silly ties,
Rodeo dreams lost at sea.

The tide rolled in like a soap opera,
Mixing laughter with splashes of fate.
With a flip-flop battle, no drama,
But the beach ball's still up for debate.

As sunset paints the sky in hues,
The crabs all share a local joke.
What do you call a tide that snooze?
A bulk in the sea, or just a bloke?

Swaying to the Island Rhythm

Grass skirts swaying, they groove and twirl,
While coconuts laugh, yeah they can jive.
Even the palm trees give it a whirl,
Hoping the sun's still alive.

A parrot squawks a birthday tune,
While tourists trip over their toes.
A ukelele plays by the moon,
As laughter lifts like the tides that rose.

The hermit crabs join in the fun,
With little soft hats and tiny shoes.
Chasing each other, oh what a run,
While beach balls puff up like big balloons.

As night blankets all in sheer delight,
Stars wink at us with a grin.
Dance till you slip and take flight,
Laughter's the key to a win!

Moonlit Walks on Sandy Shores

Booking our steps on the moon's glow,
While shadows sneak about like a thief.
Footprints tell tales we don't know,
Like a romance that snuck in with a leaf.

A crab with swagger strolls by,
As giggles float under the sky.
Seashells whisper, 'Why'd you stop there?'
But the flip-flop's lost, is that fair?

Under the stars we exchange silly tales,
Of mermaids who really can't swim.
And dolphins who go out on trails,
With fins that can sometimes go dim.

So if you stroll and hear a laugh,
It's probably from a fish in disguise.
Moonlit beaches are quite the path,
Where each shadow might just surprise.

The Call of Distant Horizons

Ahoy, matey! The wind calls low,
As wooden legs dance on the deck.
But wait—what's that? A sandcastle show?
With flags made of cotton, oh heck!

Pirates searching for rum and treasure,
Find a dolphin who's wearing a hat.
Rolling in laughter's pure pleasure,
Chasing seagulls who steal their snack.

The horizon sings of strange lands,
Where the sun likes to sip from a cup.
With tacos floating in pirate bands,
And jellyfish who just can't give up!

So join the voyage and bring your cheer,
With echoes of giggles all around.
The ocean calls, and we all hear,
That life's a treasure, silly and sound!

Whispers of the Ocean Wind

The seagulls squawk with flair,
As I try to fix my hair.
A crab scuttles at my feet,
I'm dancing to a silly beat.

My sunscreen's thick, oh what a sight,
Like a ghost in morning light.
The waves crash, water flies,
I'm making quite the splashy sighs.

Flip-flops flapping in the race,
While doing my best to keep my pace.
A fish jumps up to say hello,
I wave back, and so we go.

Laughter echoes on the shore,
As sand gets stuck in every pore.
With each gust, my hat takes flight,
The ocean breeze, what sheer delight!

Dancing Palms and Golden Sands

Palms are swaying, having fun,
They mimic me, oh what a run!
A flip-flop flies and lands nearby,
I laugh so hard, I nearly cry.

The sun's so bright, I squint my eyes,
Creating shadows and silly spies.
Shells are treasures, or so they say,
I collect them, another game to play.

A tourist wanders looking lost,
I point, but at what cost?
He ends up in the snack bar line,
With a smile, I say, "It's all divine!"

Seagulls circle, comedy in flight,
Stealing snacks, oh what a sight!
As laughter dances with the breeze,
We're all just kids with ocean tease.

Heartbeat of the Tropical Shore

The sand feels warm, I take a seat,
But ants declare a spicy treat.
They march along, a tiny parade,
While I sip juice and hope it won't fade.

My beach ball's bouncing, what a scene,
It's hit my drink, now it's a stream!
A seagull's watching with a grin,
Ready to dive, let the chaos begin!

An old man's fishing, oh so still,
But I just saw him slip and spill!
The bait that slipped leads to cheers,
He laughs it off, forgets his fears.

The waves are calling, oh what fun,
Chasing crabs, I'm not the only one.
With sun-kissed cheeks and sandy toes,
The heartbeat of the shore just glows!

Serenade of the Sea Breeze

The breeze serenades as I munch,
On coconuts, what a lunch!
A parrot squawks, "What's the deal?"
I wink and say, "I feel unreal!"

Towels wrapped like capes on me,
Flying high, just wait and see!
I spin and shout, my friend stands still,
Watching me with a thrilling chill.

Waves crash loudly with a roar,
Knocking over my drink once more.
A mermaid's laughing in the foam,
"Come and join, you're far from home!"

As evening falls and stars collide,
We pretend to surf, take a ride.
With laughter ringing through the night,
That breeze whispers tales of delight!

Enchantment of the Endless Bay

Seagulls squawk with cheeky flair,
As fishermen dance in salty air.
Tangled nets and slippery fish,
What a peculiar, soggy wish!

A crab scuttles, wearing my shoe,
While sunbathers toast to a love that's true.
Splashing kids in a water fight,
They're soggy, yes, but sheer delight!

A beach ball flies, it takes a dive,
While surfers tumble, just to survive.
Their epic fails, a comic scene,
Laughter echoes, it's a joy routine!

As sun sets low, the shore does glow,
Dancing shadows in twilight's show.
With laughter shared and smiles so bright,
Endless joys grace the starry night.

Laughter in the Warm Currents.

The sun shines down with a glint of sass,
As sunbathers tumble on the lush grass.
A floating donut, a sight so fine,
Pirates aboard, with a splash of wine!

Waves crash down, a ticklish ride,
While giggles follow the bubbling tide.
A beach ball pops, oh what a scene,
The sandy pups chase their ice-cream dream!

Old men fish with a playful pout,
While their line snags a confused trout.
"Catch a big one!" they jovially claim,
But lunch today is still quite the same!

As shadows grow long, their stories unfold,
Of tales so tall, they shimmer like gold.
With belly laughs floating in the sea,
These moments shared, forever will be.

Whispers of the Coastal Wind

The coastal breeze carries tales and jokes,
Where even a dolphin occasionally pokes.
Flip-flops flying, a wild parade,
As sunburned tourists shoulder the shade.

A seaweed wig, worn with pride,
Makes every beach bum beam and glide.
The ocean's got a funny tale,
Of snappy fish and a rogue whale!

Driftwood castles, each one unique,
A kid's imagination, oh so chic!
A crab wearing glasses, oh what a sight,
Behold the critter, read with delight!

With laughter echoing, the day's almost done,
Children chase seagulls for a bit of fun.
Under starry skies where secrets weave,
Nature's charm, a blissful reprieve.

Secrets of the Tides

When the tide rolls in, so do the clowns,
Building castles, wearing silly crowns.
Shells are treasures, a sparkly prance,
While jellyfish try a graceful dance!

A flip-flap here, a gooey splash there,
A sunfish floats, with naught a care.
As the tide retreats, it reveals the plot,
A treasure chest filled with every thought!

Sandy toes and wide-eyed glee,
A parade of laughter, both wild and free.
As the sun dips low, painting skies bright,
The secrets of the ocean parlay in the night.

The waves sing songs both brave and bold,
And silly antics are worth their weight in gold.
With starlit waters as our guide,
These tides of joy, forever abide.

Treasures Beneath the Glimmering Waves

A crab in a tux, what a sight to see,
He waltzes around with such oddity.
For pearls and riches, he digs with glee,
But only finds seaweed, quite snotty, tee hee!

The fish hold a party, it's quite the crowd,
With bubbles and laughter, they sing out loud.
A shark in a hat, feeling oh so proud,
Claims he's the DJ, he's surfy and cowed!

A turtle forgot where he left his shoe,
While seahorses giggle, they can't find it too.
They dance in the tides, oh, such a hullabaloo,
With jellyfish jiving in glow-in-the-dark blue!

The seaweed sings songs, in a slappy way,
As starfish join in for the music play.
The treasures they search, just a fun cabaret,
In depths where the silly fish laugh all day!

The Gentle Touch of Island Skies

A parrot on a branch, oh so very bright,
Repeats my own jokes, but he gets them slight.
He chuckles and squawks under the moonlight,
While coconuts fall, adding to the fright!

The sun winks down, with a cheery grin,
As I trip over roots, oh what a spin!
Tropical drink spills, now that's a win,
My laughter joins waves, let the fun begin!

A dog finds a shell, thinks it's a bone,
He buries it deep, whispers on his own.
But when it does smell, it's quite overgrown,
He snorts in disgust, oh, how he has grown!

The breezes tell tales of how we all play,
In a daring pursuit of a festive display.
With giggles and hiccups, we dance all day,
While clouds float on by, on this colorful fray!

Soothing Currents of Solitude

With a flip-flop flop and a giggle beside,
I paddle my boat, like a cork on the tide.
A sea otter waves, cheeks puffed up with pride,
As crabs dig the sand, in hasty collide!

I drift with the currents, the fish join the fun,
They swim in a conga, oh what a run!
With laughter in bubbles, the jokes are never done,
While wave-surfing dolphins shine bright in the sun!

A wild shrimp parade, they all dance around,
With sunglasses on, groovin' down to the sound.
A clam takes the stage, such talent abound,
Jokes offered by sea snails, oh they astound!

The seagrass grows wild, tickles toes in delight,
As I sip on my drink, it feels just right.
In the midst of the tides, everything feels light,
With laughter like waves crashing, a comical sight!

A Delicate Breeze Among the Palms

Bamboo sticks swinging, a hilarious sight,
As monkeys steal snacks, with pure delight.
They toss fruits around, oh what a fright,
While I dive for cover to get out of their flight!

The breeze sways the branches, they creak with a grin,
As lizards doing yoga just try to fit in.
They stretch and they pose, looking oh so thin,
While cicadas hum tunes, let's all spin!

A picnic left unattended becomes a feast,
With butterflies snacking, oh how they're pleased.
A cake starts to wiggle, and now it's released,
The ants join the party, it's sweet and beast!

The sun sets slowly, drenching the scene,
While I laugh at the chaos, oh what a routine!
In this silly saga, the best ever seen,
Among the palms swaying, life's a fun machine!

Chasing Shadows on Silver Sands

We raced with shadows on the shore,
Shouting and laughing, not keeping score.
Footprints washed away in the tide,
Chasing our laughter, there's nowhere to hide.

Seagulls were squawking, trying to play,
Stealing our snacks, then flying away.
With sand in our shoes and smiles so wide,
Building castles of dreams that dance with pride.

The sun turned our skin to toasted hue,
While we attempted to surf on dew.
Wipeouts and giggles, we fell with grace,
Emerging from splashes with foam on our face.

As sunset painted the sky with flair,
We danced like nobody else was there.
With sandy hugs and salty cheer,
Tomorrow beckons, let's do it here.

Isles of Serenity and Peace

On a tiny isle, we found our place,
Where coconuts bounced in a happy chase.
Crabs marched like soldiers, no time to spare,
Pinching our toes, they sparked a scare.

Palm trees swayed with a sassy shout,
As we tried to juggle and ended in doubt.
With every fall, we laughed even more,
Turning our mishaps into folklore.

Dancing barefoot on the sun-warmed ground,
We wiggled and giggled, made silly sounds.
With a splash on the back, we fell in the sea,
Emerging all soggy but wild and free.

Starry nights brought a magical show,
As crickets chirped in a rhythmic flow.
Toasting marshmallows with a beachy twist,
We whispered our dreams in a smoky mist.

Horizons Yet to Be Discovered

With maps made of napkins, we planned our quest,
Drawing treasure spots and scheduling rest.
We aimed for adventure with goofy delight,
Setting off giggling, ready to fight.

Splashing and hunting, we lost our way,
Found a sea turtle who joined our play.
Fishing for laughs, we caught one too,
In this ocean of jest, we just broke through.

The horizon whispered service with fries,
At a tiny café under sunny skies.
Mismatched chairs, and lemonade spills,
Every sip filled our hearts with thrills.

As the sun dipped low, our worries flew,
We twirled in circles, our joy renewed.
With dreams like treasure and hearts so light,
We packed our mischief, ready for night.

In the Embrace of Soft Breeze

The breeze played tricks, it tangled our hair,
As we tried to dance without a care.
Twisting and twirling, we looked quite absurd,
But laughter erupted, not a single word.

Sandcastles flopped, yet we cheered them on,
Armies of shells with the seagulls' dawn.
With frisbees in flight and a splash of the sea,
Our moments grew larger, wild and free.

Even the sun seemed to wink and tease,
As we gorged ourselves on the warm, sweet breeze.
Scooping up smiles and sharing the fun,
Writing our stories until day was done.

As night draped us in a blanket of stars,
We grinned at our silliness, joking bizarre.
With every step, we swirled and spun,
In the embrace of laughter, we became one.

www.ingramcontent.com/pod-product-compliance
Lightning Source LLC
Chambersburg PA
CBHW072130070526
44585CB00016B/1617